Upgrade YOUR Life TODAY

THE SECRETS TO INSTANT CHANGE

How to Rewire Your Mind for Faster Success by Building Unstoppable Confidence to Increase Your Income, Grow your Wealth, and Access the People and Opportunities most ONLY Dream About

THEODORE BASIL

Copyright © Theodore BASIL 2024

All Rights Reserved

ISBN: 978-1-7636038-3-7

No part of this publication may be reproduced, distributed, or transmitted in any form or by any means, including photocopying, recording, or other electronic or mechanical methods, without the author's prior written permission, except in the case of brief quotations embodied in critical reviews and specific other non- commercial uses permitted by copyright law.

For permission requests or business enquiries, please get in touch with the author:

Theodore Basil, directly on LinkedIn or text the word ENQUIRY directly to +61 421 781 242.

The Secrets to Instant Change

How to Rewire Your Mind, Accelerate Your Income & Transform Your Relationships — Fast!

By Theodore Basil

Chapter 1 – Why Most Information Programs Fail (And What To Do Instead)

Why the problem isn't lack of knowledge — it's lack of alignment. Most people know what to do but still don't do it because they haven't rewired the beliefs that drive their behaviour. This chapter reveals how to shift from collecting information to creating results by changing the environment, self-image, and daily structure that determine your outcomes.

Chapter 2 – Upgrade Your Circle, Elevate Your Life

Why the right people can change everything. Your environment shapes your results faster than willpower ever can. Learn how to deliberately enter "better rooms," raise your standards, and connect with high-calibre people who challenge, stretch, and accelerate your growth — because proximity is power.

Chapter 3 – Why Psychology Doesn't Work For Most People

Why awareness alone doesn't create change — and what to do instead.

This chapter exposes how traditional therapy often keeps people stuck analysing the past instead of creating the future. You'll learn a proactive model of emotional leadership built around clarity, self-talk, and identity rewiring. The focus: stop asking *"Why?"* and start asking *"What now?"*

Chapter 4 – Your Turning Point: How One Decision Can Rewrite Your Story

Real change doesn't take time — it takes a decision. Explore the moments where everything shifts: when pain becomes purpose and hesitation becomes action. You'll discover how a single, bold decision — made with conviction — can unlock more progress in weeks than years of planning ever could.

Chapter 5 – The Identity Flip: Becoming the Person Who Attracts Results Effortlessly

You don't get what you want — you get who you are. Learn the practical process of upgrading your identity to match your desired results. This chapter teaches how to act from your future self, raise your standards, and embody the version of you that naturally attracts success, wealth, and better relationships.

Chapter 6 – Empowerment Begins With You

Why does the world respond when you lead yourself first? No one is coming to save you — and that's the best news possible. This chapter gives you the tools to take back control of your confidence, focus, and influence. Learn how personal leadership builds respect, resilience, and unstoppable momentum.

Chapter 7 – Change Your Questions, Change Your Life

The fastest way to shift your thinking and influence others. You'll discover seven high-performance reframes that instantly change your focus, language, and decision-making. The right questions don't just reveal answers — they unlock clarity, creativity, and leadership energy.

Chapter 8 – The Money Truth They Never Told You

Why financial advisors can't make you wealthy — and who can. Wealth isn't about what you earn — it's about how you think. This chapter uncovers why most people outsource their financial power and how to shift from employee thinking to investor and creator thinking. Learn the real psychology behind sustainable wealth.

Chapter 9 – Influence and Income: The Power of Sales & Marketing Mastery

Without influence, your best ideas die unseen. This chapter reveals how to communicate your value, craft a clear message, and lead conversations that inspire trust. You'll learn to sell without pressure, attract aligned clients, and build authority through clarity, storytelling, and consistency.

Chapter 10 – Model the Masters: How the Top 1% Do It Differently

Success leaves clues — if you know where to look. Here, you'll uncover the thinking, routines, and philosophies of elite performers. Learn how to model excellence without imitation and shortcut years of trial and error by adopting the habits and decision frameworks of those already achieving extraordinary results.

Chapter 11 – Kill the Noise, Find Your Focus

How to reclaim your energy and attention in a distracted world. Distraction is the new addiction. This chapter shows how to cut through mental clutter, guard your attention, and create ruthless clarity around what matters most — so you can achieve more with less stress and wasted effort.

Chapter 12 – The 7-Minute Morning Reset

How to build confidence, clarity, and calm before the day begins. Learn the simple daily routine that primes your mind and energy in under seven minutes. By mastering small morning rituals, you'll create momentum that compounds into focus, productivity, and emotional balance.

Chapter 13 – Success Without Burnout

Why it's not about doing more — it's about becoming more. High performance isn't a sprint — it's a rhythm. Discover how to balance ambition with recovery, build sustainable growth without burnout, and create a lifestyle of peak performance grounded in energy, purpose, and alignment.

Chapter 14 – Your Defining Moment: The Choice That Turns Insight Into Power

Every transformation comes down to a single decision — the moment you draw a line in the sand and refuse to live the same way again. This chapter is about converting insight into action and momentum into mastery. You'll learn why waiting for the "right time" keeps most people trapped, how serendipity rewards those who are ready, and why mentorship accelerates everything. Your defining moment isn't somewhere in the future — it's the choice you make today to rise, act, and lead your life with conviction.

About Theodore Basil

Born in Brisbane to Greek migrant parents, **Theodore Basil** grew up immersed in the values of honesty, resilience, and a relentless work ethic. His parents traded city life for country towns, running small cafés in **Kerang** and **Warracknabeal**, where he learned early that success wasn't luck — it was built on **relationships, service, and trust**.

Music, though, was his first language. His grandfather, a gifted violinist, enrolled him in classical piano, teaching him discipline, rhythm, and the beauty of pattern — lessons that would later define his approach to human potential and high performance. By sixteen, Theodore had traded sonatas for stage lights, playing rock and roll in smoky pubs and eventually on stages alongside **Queen and AC/DC**. The world of music shaped his love for creativity, expression, and excellence, but also exposed him to its darker side: ***Uncertainty, Instability, and Underpayment***.

At 21 years of age, while working on the **New South Wales Central Coast**, the uncertainty of music almost cost him his life. Weak from an inadequate diet typical of a struggling musician chasing dreams, Theodore waded into the surf one afternoon, totally unaware of the powerful rip beneath the calm surface. Within moments, he was swept out to sea. As he fought to stay afloat, gasping and exhausted, one thought cut through the chaos: *"My parents won't even know I've died. No one knows where I am."*

That moment — suspended between life and death — became the **turning point**. It was clarity born from crisis. He realised he was tired of living by chance, tired of relying on luck to survive. When he finally made it back to shore, trembling but alive, he made a decision that would define the rest of his life: *he would never again depend on luck — only on growth, purpose, and self-mastery.*

He left the uncertainty of music behind and pursued a career that offered structure, accountability, and meaning. As a **financial advisor**, Theodore built a client base of over 1,000 people, conducted more than 5,000 interviews, and oversaw $120 million in managed assets. He founded a firm with 14 staff and associates generating over $5 million annually — but what fascinated him most wasn't money. It was **why some people break through while others stay stuck**.

The answer came when he met **Bob Proctor**, whose mentorship shifted everything. Proctor taught him that success wasn't about grinding harder — it was about changing how you think, expanding your awareness, and raising your standards. That was the day Theodore began mastering **the psychology of transformation** — and teaching others to do the same.

Since then, he has launched and led six successful businesses across retail, hospitality, and financial services. Today, as the founder of **Knowledge Transformation Growth (KTG)**, Theodore mentors CEOs, entrepreneurs, and professionals to rewire their mindset, grow their income, and strengthen their relationships. His life's work is distilled into a **"Success Curriculum"** — a practical framework for creating clarity, confidence, and sustainable growth.

Theodore believes the world — like music — runs on patterns. And when you learn to change those patterns, you change your results. His mission is simple yet profound: to help others break free from fear, rewrite their internal programming, and live with purpose, prosperity, and power.

"Transformation isn't just a dream. It's a conscious decision." Through clarity, courage, and new awareness, Theodore inspires others to rise beyond their limits — to live not by chance, but by design.

Table of Contents

Introduction: The Secrets to Instant Change 10

Who This Book Is For 15

Chapter 1: Why Most Information Programs Fail
— and What You Can Do Instead to Grow Your Life Results 22

Chapter 2: Upgrade Your Circle, Elevate Your Life 27

Chapter 3: The Psychology Myth 33

Chapter 4: Your Turning Point 38

Chapter 5: The Identity Flip 43

Chapter 6: Empowerment Begins with You 49

Chapter 7: Change Your Questions to Change Your Life 54

Chapter 8: The Money Truth They Never Told You 58

Chapter 9: The Importance of Sales & Marketing 62

Chapter 10: Success Leaves Clues —Here's How to Follow Them 67

Chapter 11: How to Reclaim Your Energy in a
Distracted World Drowning in Distraction 71

Chapter 12: A Simple Daily Reset for Confidence, Clarity,
and Calm Before the World Gets to You, Get to Yourself 75

CHAPTER 13: The Quiet Truth About High Achievers 80

Chapter 14: Your Defining Moment 85

The Life Success Accelerator 89

Introduction:
The Secrets to Instant Change

Most people believe that real change takes years. They've been told to be patient — to wait for life to unfold, to trust that someday the timing will be right.

But here's the truth: **lasting change doesn't depend on time — it depends on identity.**

I've seen this firsthand. As a musician who went from playing in pubs to sharing stages with legends like Queen and AC/DC, and later as a CEO who built and sold multiple businesses, I've learned that the biggest breakthroughs rarely happen slowly.

They happen in an instant — the moment you encounter a new idea, meet a new person, or adopt a new standard that forces you to see yourself differently.

One decision, one relationship, one shift in thinking can trigger a chain reaction that rewrites your entire future.

This book is about those moments — and how to create them deliberately.

You'll discover:

- Why your **environment** shapes your success more than talent ever could,
- Why **raising your standards** magnetises new opportunities, and
- Why **lottery winners often lose everything** — because they never evolved their identity to match their new reality.

Who This Book Is For

This book is for professionals, high achievers, and dreamers who feel stuck — those who've invested heavily in learning and working hard, yet sense they've hit an invisible ceiling.

It's for the person who looks successful on the outside but knows, deep down, that they're capable of *so much more.*

Maybe you're mid-career or mid-life, standing at a crossroads, quietly telling yourself:

"I know I can do better."

"I know I'm meant for more than this."

It's for the ambitious thinker who refuses to live on autopilot, and who's ready to deliberately design a life that feels bigger, bolder, and more authentic.

If you've ever felt trapped in old patterns, this book will hand you the keys to break them — not gradually, not someday, but **now.**

Once you understand the psychology of instant change — how to reprogram your mind, your relationships, and your wealth identity — you'll stop waiting for transformation and start living it.

The secrets aren't complicated, but they are uncommon. And once you see them, you can never go back.

Welcome to *The Secrets to Instant Change.*

Gratitude to My Supporters

Nobody writes a book — or changes the world — alone. My journey has been shaped by the insights, philosophies, encouragement, and belief of the remarkable people who have stood by me along the way.

- **Nobby Kleinsman** – A dear friend and fellow traveller. A former financial advisor who now calls himself a "recovering financial advisor," Nobby is dedicated to sharing his excellent program *Money Rules*, helping people master their money and take control of their financial destiny.
- **Dr. Philip Feren** – My trusted GP and close friend for more than three decades. Beyond his medical expertise, Philip has offered unwavering support through life's highs and lows — always with professionalism, compassion, and zero judgment.
- **Dr. Robert Anthony** – Acclaimed author and pioneering thinker, and one of my most treasured mentors. Our many conversations on success, human potential, and unconventional approaches to mental health were filled with wisdom, insight, and laughter.
- **Chris Pattas** – A true thought partner. With over 20 years of elite management experience, Chris has an extraordinary ability to ask the right questions — the kind that spark deep reflection and practical action.
- **Theo Golias** – My beloved brother and lifelong companion on this journey. Theo has shared in every high and low of being someone wired to take risks and challenge the status quo. Through it all, he has never stopped believing in me — even when the outcomes were uncertain.
- **Nigel Baldwin** – A close friend, regular coffee mate, and philosophical sparring partner. Our conversations often go far beyond business, exploring the deeper values that define a life truly worth living.
- **Wayne Levy** – A gifted entrepreneur and former elite tennis player whose generosity and perspective on service have deeply inspired me. Wayne's commitment to helping others succeed is one of the key reasons I am writing this book — to elevate lives and share that same spirit of contribution.

- **George Giamadakis** – My cousin and close friend. George is an accomplished executive and consultant, an inspiring leader who has built his own successful business consultancy. His guidance, wisdom, and belief have meant more than words can express.

Above all, I am eternally grateful to my beloved life partner, **Christine Pattas** — my soulmate, my anchor, and by far the most inspiring woman I have ever met. Her journey of personal success stands as an example to all who know her. Her belief in me has been unshakable, her encouragement constant, and her love the steady force that has grounded me while I've pursued my mission to help others.

My Mission Today

Helping others and making a positive difference in the world has always been my life's passion.

Today, my mission is to **inspire and guide 10,000 people over the next five years** to unlock their full potential by taking full control of their relationships, mindset, and financial future.

In these pages, I will challenge what you believe about **money, wealth, and influence**. More importantly, I'll share the patterns and principles drawn from a lifetime of study, experience, and observation — the same timeless ideas that only a small percentage of high performers truly understand, and that consistently underpin success in business, creativity, and human achievement.

I don't believe in theories that go nowhere. I believe in **action.** I believe in **measurable results.** And I believe that with the right mindset, structure, and support, **you can create the life you've always known you were capable of living.**

Connect with Me

If you'd like to collaborate on a special project or explore how we can work together, feel free to reach out:

Email: businessprofitgrowth@gmail.com

Text: Send "ENQUIRY" to **+61 421 781 242**

Who This Book Is For

This book is for the **doers** — for the professionals, leaders, and high achievers who quietly tell themselves:

"I'm capable of more than this."

It's not for the drifters, the excuse-makers, or those content to stay stuck.

It's for the **bold** — the ones ready to stop waiting and start moving.

Because here's the truth: the barrier holding you back isn't the market, the economy, or your competitors.

It's the voice in your own head telling you to stay "safe." That voice is lying.

The real ceiling stopping you is **mental** — and the moment you rewire your thinking, the game changes instantly.

In This Book, You'll Learn How To:

- Break free from stagnation and self-doubt.
- Rewire your mindset so confidence, clarity, and action become automatic.
- Create results in **weeks**, not years — through laser focus and inspired action.

I've witnessed remarkable transformations in as little as **30 to 90 days** — not because people got "lucky," but because they learned to master the only battlefield that truly matters: **their own mind.**

If you're tired of incremental progress… If you're ready for a true breakthrough…

Then this book is your manual for **instant, lasting change.**

But let's be clear:

It only works if you commit.

If you read passively, nothing will shift.

If you step in with both feet — **everything will.**

Final Word Before We Begin Our Journey

If you are:

- A professional who knows you could be achieving far more in your field.
- A high achiever who's lost momentum, hit a ceiling, and wants to accelerate forward again.
- A business founder whose growth has plateaued and is ready for a breakthrough.
- Someone who senses that life has more to offer — and is determined to discover exactly what that is.

Then you're in the right place.

This book will help you sharpen your mental edge, clarify your goals, and regain the forward motion you've been missing. It will help you step out of the comfort zone that's quietly become a trap

— and into a progressive state of living where results compound and opportunities multiply.

The choice is yours:

You can remain at the level you've already mastered, or step into the one you've been avoiding — the level that feels uncomfortable, uncertain, and, let's be honest, a little intimidating.

Every great leap in history has felt that way. So, if you're ready — **turn the page.**

Because the ceiling above you is about to become the floor you stand on.

The Secrets to Instant Change

"The world has changed! Today we are in an ideas economy, and even your best thinking from five years ago can become your baggage today."

— Daniel Priestley

The pace of change today is unlike anything humanity has ever seen. Technology is reshaping industries at lightning speed. Revolutionary ideas just a few years ago are already obsolete.

Standing still is no longer an option. Whether we like it or not, the world will continue to evolve — and if we don't evolve with it, we risk becoming irrelevant in our careers, relationships, and even in how we see ourselves.

But here's the crucial truth: **not all change is created equal. Two Types of Change**

There are two distinct kinds of change you must understand.

1. External Change

This is the change happening around you. It's automatic. It doesn't ask for your permission. Market shifts, technological breakthroughs, cultural movements, political upheavals — all of it unfolds whether you're ready or not.

You can't stop external change, but you can choose how you respond to it.

2. Internal, Intentional Change

This is the change you *choose* to create. It's the decision to grow, to learn new skills, to adopt new habits, to strengthen relationships, and to upgrade your thinking.

This is the change you control — and it's the most exciting kind, because when approached with strategy and intention, **it's limitless.**

This book is about that second kind of change — the kind that puts the power back in your hands.

3. Intentional Change

Here's the exciting part: when it comes to intentional change, **you are in control.**

You can grow, create, or achieve almost anything if you know how to think strategically, act decisively, and apply yourself resourcefully.

But let's be honest — *wanting* change isn't enough. You must know **what** you want, **why** you want it, and **how** you plan to get there.

Vague intentions like "I want to be more successful" or "I want to be happier" don't lead anywhere.

4. Success demands clarity.

When I participated in a life-changing experience called the *Accelerated Development Program*, there was one non-negotiable rule:

You couldn't join without a business plan or roadmap.

Why?

Because without direction, you can't measure progress — and without progress, motivation dies.

The same applies to life:

If you don't know your destination, **every road will feel like a dead end.**

Guidance, Support, and Accountability

One of the central truths of *The Secrets to Instant Change* is this: transformation is not a solo act — and it shouldn't be.

Across decades of working with CEOs, entrepreneurs, and high performers, I've seen one consistent pattern: people who achieve lasting breakthroughs rarely do it alone. The difference-maker isn't just motivation; it's **commitment, support, and structured accountability.**

The fastest and most sustainable change happens when three key elements are in place:

- **Guidance** – Someone who has already walked the path and can help you avoid costly mistakes, shortcuts, and dead ends.
- **Support** – A system that keeps you focused when motivation fades or life gets noisy.
- **Accountability** – A standard that won't let you slip back into old patterns without noticing — and correcting course fast.

Without these, even the best intentions fade into "someday" goals. But with them, progress becomes predictable. Momentum compounds. Change sticks.

That's why this book isn't about inspiration — it's about implementation.

You'll learn how to design your environment, habits, and mindset so that progress becomes automatic — not something you chase, but something you live.

Because real transformation doesn't happen in isolation. It happens in **structure**, in **support**, and in **deliberate action**.

So, Why Do Most People Stay Stuck for Years?

We live in an era of limitless opportunity. At our fingertips are more tools, knowledge, and connections than any generation before us. And yet, so many people feel trapped — running hard, but not moving forward.

Why?

Because **change is automatic**, but **progress is intentional**.

You don't have to do anything for your circumstances to change — time will handle that for you. Your career will evolve, your body will age, your relationships will shift, and the world will keep turning. That's change.

But progress — real, measurable improvement in your income, health, relationships, and happiness — only happens when you choose it, and when you commit to it consistently.

As Tony Robbins puts it:

"Progress is the result of conscious thought, decision, and action."

Most people delay those decisions. They wait for the "right time" or for motivation to strike. They say they'll begin after the holidays, once the kids are older, when work slows down, or when life feels easier.

But the truth is simple: **you will never feel ready.**

Progress doesn't wait for perfect conditions — it begins the moment you decide to act despite them.

Bridging the Gap

The Secrets to Instant Change is your roadmap to close the gap between where you are and where you want to be — faster than you think possible.

In these pages, you'll discover how to:

- Create a crystal-clear vision of your future.
- Build the mindset and habits that make progress inevitable.
- Break through emotional and mental barriers that have held you back for years.
- Attract high-quality relationships that open doors you didn't even know existed.
- Stay accountable when life tests your focus and resolve.

Most importantly, you'll learn how to create **change that lasts** — the kind that becomes part of your identity, not just a short-lived burst of effort.

Is This You?

Have you ever found yourself:

- Starting strong but losing momentum,
- Knowing what to do but not following through,
- Feeling capable of more but unsure how to get there…

If any of these sound familiar, this book is written for you.

You Are the Author of Your Next Chapter

Your future isn't defined by your past — it's defined by your next decision.

You already have more influence over your life than you realise. But influence without direction leads nowhere. You need clarity, strategy, and the right allies walking beside you.

That's what *The Secrets to Instant Change* is about: designing transformation instead of waiting for it, and surrounding yourself with the guidance, support, and accountability to make it last.

Because here's the truth — no one can do your push-ups for you. The work is yours. But with the right structure, you'll find yourself doing that work with focus, consistency, and a renewed sense of purpose.

So take a breath.

Turn the page.

Because the next chapter of your life begins now.

Chapter 1:
Why Most Information Programs Fail — and What You Can Do Instead to Grow Your Life Results

The Real Reason You're Stuck Isn't What You Think

You've bought the courses. You've filled shelves with books.

You've sat through the seminars, taken pages of notes, and filed them neatly in binders.

And yet… it still feels like you're pushing a boulder uphill.

If you've ever thought, *"Why am I not further ahead? I already know all this stuff,"* you're not alone.

I've met CEOs, consultants, and seasoned entrepreneurs who can quote personal-development principles word for word—sometimes better than the authors themselves. Yet their results don't match their knowledge.

It's not laziness.

It's not a lack of drive. It's not intelligence.

The reason runs deeper.

The Weekend That Changed Everything

Thirty years ago, I attended my first professional-development seminar: **"You Were Born Rich"** with Bob Proctor.

At the time, I was three years into my financial-advisory career. On paper, I was doing fine—bills paid, modest client base, respectable progress. But deep down, I knew I was leaving potential on the table.

That weekend flipped the switch.

Yes, the content was excellent. We worked through Bob's full U.S. program, workbook in hand. His famous *goal card*—a pocket-sized reminder of your vision—became my daily companion.

But the real magic wasn't the information. It was the **environment**.

There were seven of us in that room. Within 30 days, every one of us had achieved extraordinary results. My own income skyrocketed more than 300 per cent within a year—not because of a new tactic, but because I started operating differently.

Bob gave me one piece of advice that has stayed with me ever since:

"Schedule your first client at 9 a.m. at least four days a week. Once a week, take a high-level contact out for breakfast. Don't sell— learn. Ask about their expertise. Understand what drives them."

That single habit changed everything. My mornings had purpose.

My conversations had depth.

My self-image shifted—I stopped trying to *be* a financial advisor and started *acting* like a high-level one.

And my results rose to meet that standard.

The lesson: the right environment, paired with structured action, creates breakthroughs faster than most people believe possible.

The Myth of "If I Know It, I'll Do It"

We've all been told that *knowledge is power.*

It isn't.

Knowledge without application is like owning a Ferrari with no fuel— impressive in the driveway, useless on the road.

If information alone were enough, nobody would be overweight, broke, or stuck in unfulfilling work.

Today, information is everywhere—podcasts, YouTube, courses, articles— yet most people still fail to change.

Why?

Because over 90 per cent of your actions are driven not by conscious thought, but by habits and beliefs buried in your **subconscious**.

Your conscious mind can learn something in hours. Your subconscious—the part that learned its deepest patterns before you were seven—runs the show.

Highlighting a passage in a book won't rewrite those programs. They change only when you **deliberately rewire them**.

The Comfort-Zone Trap

Every time you attempt a big leap—a business, a fitness goal, a financial stretch—your subconscious asks one question: *"Is this familiar?"*

If the answer is no, it resists. Not because it wants you to fail, but because its job is to keep you safe.

The "known," even if it's miserable, feels secure. The "unknown," even if it's better, feels dangerous.

That's why people stay in jobs they hate, why entrepreneurs cling to outdated strategies, and why teams settle for mediocrity. The comfort zone isn't comfortable—it's a cage.

Why Most Programs Fail

Here's the industry's dirty little secret: most self-improvement programs train only your **conscious** mind.

They hand you frameworks, tools, and tactics—but never upgrade the operating system underneath.

It's like giving someone a Formula One car without teaching them how to drive. They stall, crash, or burn out long before the finish line.

That's why people leave a seminar inspired, only to fall back into old patterns within weeks.

Why This Book Is Different

This isn't about piling on more information.

It's about **rewiring your mental software** so you automatically take the right actions—without constant battles of willpower.

It's about moving from **Reasons Mode**—where you justify staying stuck—into **Results Mode**, where you take ownership and create turning points on demand.

We'll start with *mind-management mastery*: reshaping your self-image, rewiring your thought patterns, and reprogramming your identity. Once that inner shift locks in, external success follows naturally.

Real-World Transformations

I've seen this play out hundreds of times:

- **The Stalled CEO** – Revenue flat for three years. After adopting a "decision-sprint" morning routine and a new peer environment, his company closed its biggest deal in a decade within six weeks.
- **The Burnt-Out Consultant** – Knew every productivity hack but lived in 80-hour weeks. By shifting her identity from "busy expert" to "strategic leader," she doubled her income while halving her hours.
- **The Young Entrepreneur** – Thought he needed more marketing knowledge. What he really needed was the courage to sell. After reframing his beliefs about selling, he signed three high-ticket clients in 30 days.

Their breakthroughs didn't come from *new* information—only from a *new* identity.

Why Environment Accelerates Change

When you surround yourself with people already playing at the level you aspire to, your subconscious recalibrates.

That's what I experienced in Bob Proctor's seminar. We weren't just learning—we were transforming together.

When success becomes normal in your environment, your brain resets its baseline.

That's why in my **Results vs Reasons** program; the group dynamic is as critical as the material.

The environment is the multiplier. It accelerates identity change and makes new standards stick.

Are You Ready to Change Your Life Today?

If you're still reading, you already feel it—you've outgrown your current level.

This book will show you how to:
- Break autopilot habits that keep you stuck.
- Install empowering thought patterns that make success natural.
- Act decisively without second-guessing.
- Build an environment that lifts you higher.
- Create turning points on demand—instead of waiting for "someday."

The choice is simple:

Stay in **Reasons Mode** and defend the status quo… Or step boldly into **Results Mode**, rewire your mind, and make rapid change your new normal.

Your next chapter starts now.

Chapter 2:
Upgrade Your Circle, Elevate Your Life

Why the Right People Can Change Everything

"You are the average of the five people you spend the most time with."

Jim Rohn

"The only way to raise the quality of your life and improve your results is to begin to raise your standards."

Tony Robbins

If there's one truth I've witnessed again and again — in business, leadership, and life — it's this: **success is contagious, and so is stagnation.**

You inevitably become like the people you spend the most time with. Their standards become your standards. Their limitations become your limitations. Their habits shape your own.

Spend time with small thinkers and excuse-makers, and you'll unconsciously mirror their energy. Spend time with driven, responsible, high achievers, and your expectations rise automatically — not because you're forcing yourself to improve, but because excellence becomes your baseline.

That's why I often say:

You don't rise to your goals — you fall to your environment.

The Program That Changed My Career

One of the most defining experiences of my career wasn't a seminar or a course — it was being accepted into the **AMP Accelerated Advisor Development Program (AADP).**

At that time, I was already performing well as a financial advisor. But this program didn't just make me better; it completely **redefined my standards.**

Only 12 advisors from across the country were selected each year. It wasn't a program for those who *wanted to improve a little.* You had to qualify. You had to prove results. You had to be ready to play at a higher level.

Each participant had to submit a **12-month business plan**, grounded in real numbers — last year's sales, revenue, and growth targets. No vague goals. No motivational slogans. You had to lay your track record on the table and **commit to outperforming it.**

That single act — putting real results in writing — raised the bar for everyone in the room. It created an environment where accountability wasn't optional; it was oxygen.

But the real transformation wasn't in the numbers. It was in the circle.

These were some of the top performers in the country. Every conversation, every meeting, every shared challenge stretched my thinking. Their success reframed what I believed was possible. I began to absorb their standards by osmosis.

When the program ended, I left not only with strategies, but with a new identity.

I wasn't "trying" to grow anymore. I was surrounded by people for whom growth was the only acceptable state.

And that's when Tony Robbins' quote hit home:

"The only way to raise the quality of your life and improve your results is to begin to raise your standards."

That's exactly what the AADP did for me.

Gary's Turning Point

Years later, I saw this same principle change someone else's life.

Gary was a real estate agent earning about $80,000 a year. His marriage was strained by financial pressure. He wasn't lazy or unskilled — he was simply **stuck**.

When Gary joined one of my *Results vs. Reasons* workshops, he didn't just sit quietly in the back. He immersed himself. He surrounded himself with people who were thinking bigger, aiming higher, and living by stronger standards.

Through those conversations, Gary realised he had untapped potential within his Jewish heritage community. He began collaborating with accountants and financial professionals in that network, building partnerships that created a steady stream of high- quality clients.

Within two years, Gary's income had grown to over **$650,000.** But the real transformation wasn't financial. His marriage healed. His confidence skyrocketed. His entire sense of possibility expanded.

Gary didn't just learn new tactics — he **changed his circle**, and that changed everything.

The Two Levers of Change

Every meaningful turning point in life comes down to two levers:
1. A **new person or idea** enters your life.
2. That encounter sparks a **new belief or behaviour** within you.

That's it.

You don't need another year of grinding — you need new *exposure.* New people, new ideas, and new standards that make your old ones impossible to accept.

That's why upgrading your circle is the fastest way to upgrade your life.

The Hidden Cost of Staying the Same

Here's the thing: the cost of staying in the wrong circle doesn't always look like failure.

Sometimes, it looks like *comfortable success* — a decent career, a steady income, a life that's fine... but flat.

That's the danger of mediocrity: it disguises itself as stability.

I've seen brilliant professionals stall not because they lacked talent, but because **no one around them demanded more.** They became the biggest fish in a small pond — and the pond itself became their ceiling.

Growth doesn't happen in isolation. It happens in **proximity** — proximity to people who stretch you, challenge you, and refuse to let you play small.

Growth with Integrity

Upgrading your circle doesn't mean cutting people off or creating drama. It's about **elevating your influence with intention.**

Here's how to do it with integrity:
1. **Get clear on what your next level needs.** What kind of thinking, energy, or accountability does it require?
2. **Enter the right rooms.** Seek masterminds, communities, and environments where high standards are normal.
3. **Add value first.** Approach with curiosity, not neediness. Contribute before you expect returns.
4. **Let old ties fade naturally.** Some connections won't follow your growth. That's okay.
5. **Raise the rent mentally.** Decide what kind of mindset earns space in your inner circle.

This isn't about becoming someone else — it's about surrounding yourself with people who bring out the best in who you already are.

Turning Points Don't Just Happen

Think back to your life's key turning points:
- A mentor challenged you to level up.
- A peer's success made you realise you could do more.
- A conversation shifted your entire outlook.

Those moments weren't luck. They were *engineered* by being in the right environments.

High achievers don't wait for inspiration — they **design conditions for transformation.**

They know that breakthroughs don't come from more time; they come from better circles.

Are You Ready to Upgrade Your Circle?

If you feel plateaued — in business, income, or fulfilment — it may be because your circle has become too small, too comfortable, or too predictable.

The good news? You're one decision away from changing that.

Choose better rooms. Seek higher standards. Surround yourself with people who make excellence feel normal.

When you upgrade your circle, you don't just gain new opportunities.

You gain a new identity.

Chapter Summary — Top 5 Takeaways

1. **Environment shapes the result more than intention.** You don't rise to your goals — you fall to your surroundings.
2. **Identity shifts before income shifts.** Who you believe you are determines how you show up.
3. **Turning points are engineered.** Step intentionally into rooms that stretch you.
4. **Growth requires integrity.** Elevating your circle means raising standards, not cutting ties.
5. **You're one decision away.** Choose your circle wisely — your next level depends on it.

Chapter 3:
The Psychology Myth

How to Look After and Strengthen Your Mental Health and Why Traditional Therapy Can Keep You Stuck

Modern psychology often focuses on analysis rather than action. It fosters insight but rarely delivers transformation.

This chapter exposes its limitations and introduces a **proactive model** for mastering your mental health, emotional resilience, and identity—without staying trapped in the past.

Why Most Mental Health Models Keep You Stuck

Have you ever asked yourself:

"Why do I feel this way?"

It seems logical. After all, we're trained to ask this question—from parents, teachers, therapists, and self-help books. If we want to fix a problem, we're told, first understand it.

So we dig into our past. We search for reasons. We revisit childhood events, dissect trauma, analyse relationships, and replay conversations—hoping insight alone will bring change.

Here's the truth most people don't admit:

Knowing why something happened rarely moves you forward. For many, it keeps them trapped in an endless loop of overthinking. **Why I Abandoned the Traditional Therapy Model**

As a psychotherapist, I spent three years working within the traditional model: listening, reframing, and digging deep into the past. I wanted to help people uncover the root of their struggles.

Over time, I realised something critical: **this model kept people stuck.**

Too much energy went into reliving old stories instead of creating new ones. And then it hit me:

If we keep replaying the old movie, we never make space for the new one.

From that moment, I steered clients — and myself — away from the archives. I rarely revisit old memories. They're filed away as "past movies."

Why? Because I prefer **producing new stories**—stories of possibility, challenge, and excitement that I'm directing right now.

The Hidden Shortcoming in Modern Psychology

Many study psychology to understand the "why" of their pain. They gain awareness and empathy for themselves and others.

But after years of coaching, I noticed a pattern: Clients would talk week after week about the same problems. They gained insight, articulated their feelings, but **nothing changed.**

They were becoming **experts in their problems**, not experts in solving them.

Modern therapy fosters **awareness** but neglects **action**. It encourages labelling, not leadership. Insight without implementation rarely transforms a life.

Why Asking "Why" Can Keep You Stuck

Your mind is a search engine. Ask, *"Why am I unhappy?"* and it pulls up every betrayal, failure, and disappointment from your past.

Not to hurt you—but because you asked.

The problem: you reinforce the very state you want to escape. The same story, the same memories, the same emotions. Your brain begins to believe that loop **is who you are.**

The shift:

Instead of asking *"Why?"*, ask **"What now?" The Power of "What Now?"**

Old question: Why did this happen to me?

New question: What can I do now to change this?

This simple pivot moves you from **reflection to action**, from victimhood to ownership.

It's not that exploring the past is wrong—sometimes it's necessary, especially for trauma. But for most people, the problem isn't insight—it's **momentum**.

They don't need another year of therapy. They need a new way of thinking. They need to **lead themselves.**

The Client Who Broke Free

One of my clients, Daniel (name changed), had years of therapy behind him. He read every self-help book and journaled weekly. And yet… his life wasn't moving forward.

His self-talk kept him imprisoned:
- "I can't help feeling this way."
- "I'm broken because of what happened."
- "Until I figure it out, I can't be happy."

We flipped the script. I taught him to **notice and interrupt old language patterns** and replace them with ownership statements:
- "I'm in charge of my mental state."
- "What happened shaped me, but it doesn't define me."
- "I can choose a different focus right now."

Next, we practised **mental rest**. Daniel had never meditated. We started with short sessions of **no-thought states**—simply silence, no visualisation, no analysis.

For the first time in years, his nervous system found stillness. This became his **reset button**. Over weeks, calm became his default. His relationships improved. His productivity rose. And most importantly, he **lived differently**.

Becoming Your Own Therapist

You can't outsource emotional leadership. Guidance and tools help—but the responsibility is yours.

Ask yourself:

- Is this thought helping me or hurting me?
- What am I choosing to focus on right now?
- What can I do in the next 10 minutes to shift this?

Using these questions builds **emotional self-sufficiency**. You stop waiting for someone else to change your life—you start **directing it yourself.**

Breaking the Victim Loop

It's easy to default to blame:

- "My parents never believed in me."
- "My ex betrayed me."
- "My boss doesn't value me."

True, these events may have happened. But assigning your suffering to others **gives away your power.** The exit door? **Responsibility.**

The Language of Power

The way you speak shapes your mental state:

- "She ruined my self-esteem" → Someone else controls your worth.
- "I'm rebuilding my confidence" → Your brain engages to make it real.

Change your language, change your state.

The New Model for Mental Strength

Shift from victimhood to ownership:

- Failures become **feedback**, not identity.
- Challenges become **training**, not punishment.
- The past becomes a **reference**, not a residence.

You don't need another perfect day to start. You don't need another book.

You need a decision to **lead yourself**.

Chapter Summary – Top 5 Takeaways

1. **Insight isn't enough.** Knowing why you feel a certain way doesn't guarantee change—action does.
2. **Stop asking "Why?"** Shift to "What now?" to move from reflection to progress.
3. **Live in the present.** File past events as "old movies" and create new ones.
4. **Learn mental rest.** Practice "no-thought" states to reset and calm your nervous system.
5. **Take ownership.** Your emotions are your responsibility; stop outsourcing your inner leadership.

Chapter 4:
Your Turning Point

One Bold Decision Can Shatter Years of Stagnation

Some moments change everything—not gradually, but instantly. They strike like lightning, and from that point forward, nothing is the same.

One of those moments happened for me at a live session with Phillip Guest, one of Australia's most respected financial planners. Trusted by high-profile clients—celebrities, elite sportspeople—Phillip wasn't just sharing tactics. He was revealing a mindset of preparation, trust, and discipline.

At the time, I was three years into my financial advisory career. On paper, things looked fine: bills paid, modest client base, business ticking the boxes. Inside, I felt restless. I was coasting.

Phillip's formula was simple—but revolutionary for me:
1. **Start with the client interview.** Sit them down, ask the right questions, capture everything—assets, income, concerns, dreams. Let your assistant take meticulous notes.
2. **Design a tailored plan.** Build a strategy covering risk management, investment growth, wealth building, and lifestyle needs.
3. **Structure for the long game.** For athletes, this meant protecting assets and building retirement security beyond the spotlight.

I left that session and made a **non-negotiable decision**: I would adopt the same discipline. Stop winging it. Start operating like a top-tier professional.

Within months, my numbers climbed. Within a year, my income rose by over 300%. More importantly, **my identity changed**. I no longer acted like someone "getting by." I was serving at the top of the industry.

This was my **Peripeteia**—a dramatic turning point. And over the years, I've seen countless clients experience similar breakthroughs.

The Psychology of a Turning Point

The ancient Greeks called it **Peripeteia**: a sudden reversal of fortune.

In real life, it's rarely random. It's triggered by **a non-negotiable decision**. Not "I'll try." Not "We'll see." But:

"This changes today. No debate."

Identity shifts first, actions follow. As Gary Ryan Blair notes, deciding who you are is one of the most underused forces in human potential.

Case Study: Virginia's Breakthrough

Virginia, a financial planner with 15 years of experience, had a stalled business. Her marketing relied on outdated tactics: cold calls, weak LinkedIn posts, and ineffective seminars. Client meetings followed a tired script, focusing on her credentials rather than listening.

When we engaged, we focused on two things:

1. **Rebuilding client conversations.** High-value, fact-finding meetings to uncover real financial and emotional drivers. Questions first, solutions second.
2. **Modernizing marketing.** Targeted digital campaigns with messaging that spoke directly to her ideal clients.

Results:

- 28% jump in new client revenue in 90 days.
- 40% increase over 12 months.
- Shifted from chasing clients to **attracting them naturally**.
- Rebuilt her identity from "planner" to **trusted problem solver and thought leader**.

Her turning point wasn't tactics—it was a decision to step into a new identity.

Micro Turning Points Matter

Not all turning points are dramatic. Small shifts compound when backed by a bold decision.

Example: A business coach invited a local entrepreneur to breakfast. That meeting led to an introduction to a CEO, which led to a keynote engagement, landing six high-value clients.

Investment: Four breakfasts.

Impact: A completely new trajectory. **Why Most People Never Reach This** It's not laziness. It's conditioning.

We're trained to wait for the "right time," avoid discomfort, and procrastinate. But change doesn't wait. Moving to a new environment, job, or relationship won't help if you carry the same beliefs and habits.

Real achievers reach a point where **the pain of staying the same exceeds the pain of change**. That's when everything flips.

The Two Kinds of Pain

Gary Ryan Blair: "Everything you want in life comes with a price tag. That price is suffering."

Which pain will you choose?

- **The pain of discipline:** Early mornings, tough calls, awkward conversations, investment in growth.
- **The pain of regret:** Years later, knowing you could have done more but didn't.

After Phillip Guest's session, I embraced the pain of discipline— and avoided the pain of regret entirely.

The Ripple Effect of One Decision

A turning point spreads:

- Income increases, but so does self-image.
- Confidence grows, creating trust in others.
- Opportunities appear that were invisible before.

Virginia's new marketing generated leads, but her **confidence in conversations** created trust, closing deals and generating momentum.

It all starts with **one bold, non-negotiable choice**. **Your Peripeteia Could Be Today**

You know where you're holding back. You know what behaviors no longer serve you.

Stop waiting for a "perfect moment." There isn't one. Turning points are **chosen, not stumbled upon**.

It could be as simple as:

- Committing to a new habit for 30 days.
- Ending a tolerated behavior.
- Saying yes to a mentor, program, or investment that scares you in a good way.

It doesn't need fireworks—it just needs to be **real**. **The Challenge**

1. Identify **one decision** you've been avoiding.
2. Commit to it within the next **24 hours**.
3. Act immediately—before doubt talks you out of it.

Write the date down. Circle it. This could be your Peripeteia.

Chapter Summary — 5 Key Takeaways

1. **Turning points are created by you.** Start with a non-negotiable decision.
2. **Identity shifts before results.** Change how you see yourself, actions follow.
3. **Discipline beats regret.** The pain of change is temporary; regret lasts a lifetime.
4. **Small, consistent actions compound.** One breakfast, one conversation, one habit at a time.
5. **Start now.** Your moment could be today—don't wait for the "perfect time."

Chapter 5:
The Identity Flip

How to Become the Person Who Attracts Great Results Effortlessly

Change isn't about doing more — it's about **becoming someone else**.

You can't solve your biggest problems with the same thinking, habits, and self-image that created them. You can't attract higher-paying clients, healthier relationships, or bigger opportunities while still seeing yourself as the person who struggles to deserve them.

Jim Rohn put it best:

"To HAVE more or DO more, you first have to BE more by growing yourself into becoming a more attractive person."

The **Identity Flip** is exactly that — a deliberate transformation of who you believe yourself to be, so the results you want become inevitable.

This isn't "faking it until you make it." It's **embodying the identity of your future self** until success becomes your default state.

Why Identity Shapes Everything

Everything in life — income, relationships, health, influence — is a reflection of **who you believe yourself to be**, not who you say you are.

- See yourself as average → make average decisions.
- See yourself as a leader → act in ways that command respect.
- See yourself as someone who attracts wealth → gravitate toward the habits and environments that deliver it.

The mistake most people make: **focusing on what to do instead of who to be.**

Typical goals:

- Earn an extra $50,000 this year
- Lose 10 kg
- Meet a new partner
- Get promoted

Missing question:

"Who would I need to become for these results to feel normal?"

When you change identity first, actions follow naturally.

Raising Your Price Tag

Jim Rohn often spoke about **putting a higher price on yourself** — not arrogantly, but in recognition of your standards, time, and value.

Think about it: if you valued your time at $500/hour, would you:

- Hit snooze for extra sleep?
- Scroll social media for hours?
- Sit in low-value meetings?

Of course not.

Raising your personal "price tag" isn't just about charging more — it's about **seeing your life, attention, and energy as premium**.

Example: James, the Consultant Who Doubled His Rates

James had been charging the same rate for years. Overworked, underpaid, burning out.

I asked:

"If you were the highest-priced consultant in your field, how would you act differently?"

His response: prepare more thoroughly, be selective with clients, invest in skills at a higher level.

Next week, we doubled his rates. Immediate effects:
- Posture and confidence improved
- Meetings sharper, more focused
- Within a month, landed two clients at the higher rate

What changed first wasn't his business model — it was his identity.

How the Identity Flip Works

The Identity Flip is a **three-stage process**:
1. **Define Your Future Self** – Detail how your future self thinks, handles challenges, and what standards they refuse to compromise.
2. **Act "As If" — with Integrity** – Align actions with your future self. If they're disciplined with money, track spending now. If they're confident in sales, start practicing today.
3. **Reinforce with Environment** – Surround yourself with people, rooms, and conversations that support your new self.

Operating from your future identity closes the gap between where you are and where you want to be.

Why People Resist the Identity Flip

Because it's uncomfortable.

Your old identity is familiar, even if it produces mediocre results. Safety feels better than progress.

Self-sabotage occurs when people step into their future self briefly, then retreat because it feels awkward.

Winners **push through discomfort**, allowing the new identity to take hold.

Example: Sarah, the Business Owner Who Had to Fire Herself

Sarah ran a small marketing agency. CEO on paper, but a "hardworking freelancer" in reality.

We asked:

"If you were the CEO of a $5M agency, what would you do differently?"

Actions:

- Hired a project manager
- Stopped doing low-level tasks
- Focused on partnerships

Results:

- Tripled business development activity within a month
- Revenue doubled within a year
- Her hours didn't double — her **identity did**

Building the Beliefs of Your Future Self

Results flow from actions, and actions flow from **beliefs**.

Ask yourself:
- What beliefs does my future self hold about money, success, and opportunity?
- Which current beliefs contradict that vision?
- How can I replace them with empowering beliefs?

Jim Rohn: "Don't wish it was easier, wish you were better."

The Identity Flip is about **becoming the person who thrives, regardless of conditions**.

Raising Standards, Raising Results

Your identity sets your **standards**, and your standards set your results.
- Tolerate missed deadlines → continue attracting them
- Demand excellence → attract high performers

"You are the average of the five people you spend the most time with." Upgrade your identity → naturally upgrade your circle.

The Feedback Loop of the Identity Flip

Magic happens when results reinforce identity:
1. Act like a high performer
2. Get better results
3. See yourself as a high performer
4. Act like one even more

The loop becomes self-sustaining. **The hardest part is the first step** — acting before you feel ready.

Your Turn: The Identity Audit
1. Write down your **current identity** in detail.
2. Write down your **desired identity** — the person with the results you want.
3. Identify **gaps** — habits, standards, beliefs, associations.
4. Act from your new identity immediately in at least one area.

It's about **alignment, not perfection**.

Final Word

The Identity Flip isn't pretending. It's **stepping into your most powerful, capable self** and letting results catch up.

You don't attract success by chasing it — you attract it by **becoming the kind of person for whom success is natural**.

To have more or do more, you must first **be more**. Raise your standards. Raise your price tag. Raise your identity. Everything else will follow.

Chapter 6:
Empowerment Begins with You

No One Is Coming to Save You

It might sound blunt, but it's true. Too many people wait for the "right economy," the "right boss," or the "right partner" to solve their problems.

The truth: the quality of your life begins with the standards you set for yourself.

If you outsource your power, you give up your potential. If you lead yourself first, the world can't help but respond.

Stop Outsourcing Your Power

It's easy to let your mood, confidence, or success depend on others:
- Your mood depends on someone else's opinion
- Your income depends on your employer
- Your self-worth depends on social media likes

Every time you do this, you shrink.

Tony Robbins: "It's not the events of our lives that shape us, but our beliefs about what those events mean."

Reclaiming your power is about **choosing your response**, not letting the outside world dictate your story.

The Moment You Decide to Lead Yourself

I've seen it countless times: the moment someone stops waiting for permission and starts leading themselves, everything changes.

Example: Michael, Senior Executive

- High salary, corner office, yet constant stress.
- Team underperforming, felt unsupported.

Instead of searching for management hacks, we focused on **personal leadership**: standards, clarity, and state.

Result:
- His posture and energy shifted
- Conversations became clear and impactful
- Team performance improved, **not because they changed, but because he did**

Lesson: Lead yourself first — external change follows.

Why the World Responds to Certainty

Humans are drawn to **certainty, not arrogance**.
- Confidence signals competence; people trust it.
- Hesitation signals doubt; opportunities vanish.

Certainty starts within. When you embody it, the world reflects it.

Case Study: Anna's Reset

Anna, a consultant, was exhausted: chasing clients, discounting services, anxious about being "good enough."

We started with **identity and self-leadership**, not strategy.

Question: "If you were the kind of consultant clients line up to work with, how would you show up?"

Answer: Stop discounting, set boundaries, project confidence.

Outcome:
- Raised rates by 30%
- Replaced low-value clients with high-value ones
- Worked from a place of **self-respect, not desperation**

Lesson: Empowerment changes the way the market responds.

The Trap of Waiting

Most people stay stuck waiting:
- For the economy to improve
- For recognition from a boss
- For someone else to notice their potential

The truth: **nobody is as invested in your life as you are**. Stop waiting. Start leading.

The Three Pillars of Self-Leadership

To lead yourself first, master three pillars:

1. Clarity of Standards

- Decide what you will no longer tolerate — in yourself, others, and your results.
- Write it down. Draw the line. Standards are the foundation of empowerment.

2. Consistency of State

- Your emotional state drives behavior.
- Morning routines, meditation, journaling, or fitness — whatever centers you, make it non-negotiable.

3. **Courage in Action**
   - Fear never disappears, but courage grows when you act anyway.
   - Lead yourself by tackling what you've been avoiding. Fear shrinks the moment you act.

Master these pillars, and you won't need to demand respect — it will naturally follow.

Why People Follow Leaders Who Lead Themselves

Humans calibrate to the strongest energy in the room.
- Grounded, confident, clear → others rise
- Scattered, uncertain, defensive → others sink

Leadership begins with **self-leadership**. Energy precedes influence.

Example: The Advisor Who Stopped Playing Small

Daniel had undercharged for years, feeling "lucky to have clients." We shifted his identity: **high-value advisor**.

Results:
- Raised fees
- Trimmed low-value clients
- Doubled revenue within a year
- Empowered and confident, no longer begging for business

Lesson: Lead with value and certainty — the market responds.

Empowerment Is Contagious

When you raise yourself:
- Clients respect you more
- Teams follow your lead
- Relationships improve
- Opportunities expand

Empowerment spreads. Model courage and standards, and others rise with you.

Your Call to Action

Identify areas where you've been **outsourcing your power**. Decide today:
1. One standard you'll raise
2. One state-management habit you'll commit to
3. One courageous action you'll take in the next 24 hours

Lead yourself first — watch how quickly the world responds.

Chapter Summary — 5 Key Takeaways

1. **Stop outsourcing your power** — your response, not circumstances, shapes your life.
2. **The world responds to certainty** — lead yourself first, others follow.
3. **Empowerment begins with standards** — decide what you will no longer tolerate.
4. **Self-leadership creates influence** — people calibrate to your energy before your words.
5. **Empowerment is contagious** — raise yourself, and those around you rise too.

Chapter 7:
Change Your Questions to Change Your Life

Ask Better Questions, Change Your Life

One of the fastest ways to transform results is deceptively simple:

ask better questions.

Questions drive focus. Focus drives decisions. Decisions shape destiny.

Most people believe life is shaped by the answers they get. It isn't. Life is shaped by the questions they ask themselves—and others— every day.

Tony Robbins: "Successful people ask better questions, and as a result, they get better answers."

Dale Carnegie: "The most magnetic person in the room is the one who shows genuine interest in others before others become interested in you."

The quality of your life is truly reflected in the quality of your questions.

Why Questions Matter More Than Answers

Consider this:

- Ask, *"Why am I always broke?"* → your brain delivers a depressing list of reasons.
- Ask, *"How can I double my income in 12 months?"* → your brain starts scanning for solutions.

Same brain. Different question. Entirely different trajectory.

Questions are like GPS for your subconscious:

- *Why me?* → spirals into excuses
- *What's next?* → scans for opportunity

The Secret to Connecting Instantly With Others

Whether at an event, with a client, or online, **trust is built through the questions you ask**.

Most people default to scripts, trying to pitch before earning attention. Conversations fall flat.

Carnegie's principle still holds: **be interested in others before expecting interest in you**.

Focus on four priorities most people care about:
1. **Family** – children, parents, life influences
2. **Occupation** – work, career journey, ambitions
3. **Recreation** – hobbies, passions, travel
4. **Philosophy** – values, worldview, beliefs

Guide conversations toward these areas, and trust opens naturally.

The 7 Mental Reframe Questions

Shift your inner dialogue and your conversations with these high-performance reframes:

1. **From "What do I want?" → "Who do I want to become?"**
   Results follow identity. Stop chasing tactics—embody the person who naturally achieves them.
2. **From "What do I say to impress?" → "What can I ask to understand?"**
   Replace performance pressure with curiosity. People light up when they feel heard.
3. **From "Why isn't this working?" → "What can I learn from this?"**
   Shift from victimhood to growth. Failure becomes fuel, not final.
4. **From "How do I sell this?" → "How do I solve their problem?"**
   Great salespeople serve first. Solutions naturally follow.

5. **From "What's in it for me?" → "How can I add value here?"**
   Contribution builds reputation faster than self-promotion. Doors open when you deliver value.
6. **From "Do I have the time?" → "Is this the highest use of my time?"**
   Reframe busyness into priority. Cut noise. Elevate impact.
7. **From "What will they think of me?" → "How can I make them feel?"**
   Influence comes from significance, not impressiveness.

The Client Conversation Shift

Imagine sitting across from a potential client. Most advisors launch into a monologue. The better approach? **Flip the spotlight**.

- **Occupation:** "How did you get into this line of work?"
- **Family:** "Who's been most influential in your journey?"
- **Recreation:** "What do you do to recharge outside work?"
- **Philosophy:** "What's the most important thing to get right in the next few years?"

You're not interrogating—you're unlocking stories. When someone feels heard, trust builds naturally.

A Personal Lesson in Asking Better Questions

I once interviewed a panel of financial experts. Generic questions produced surface-level answers.

When I asked: *"What was your biggest mistake in your first year, and how did you recover?"*, the room came alive.

Lesson: Curiosity is currency. It buys access to insights, stories, and trust you'd never get otherwise.

The Courage to Ask

Most people avoid asking meaningful questions—afraid of seeming intrusive or being rejected.

But people are waiting for someone to care enough to ask. They're longing for someone to uncover their story.

Asking great questions is **not a tactic—it's leadership**. It's the bridge from strangers to partners, from surface chatter to life- changing opportunities.

Chapter Summary — 5 Key Takeaways

1. **Your life follows your questions.** Better questions create better direction.
2. **Curiosity builds connection.** Show genuine interest first.
3. **FORe Framework matters.** Family, Occupation, Recreation, Philosophy are universal rapport-builders.
4. **Seven reframes shift identity.** Focus on becoming, learning, solving, adding value, and prioritising impact.
5. **Ask boldly.** Courage to ask meaningful questions separates leaders from the crowd.

Chapter 8:
The Money Truth They Never Told You

Money Is Simple. People Are Complicated.

Over my 15-year career as a financial advisor, I discovered a truth most people never do: **money is simple, but people are complicated.**

You can learn compound interest, balance sheets, or investment options in hours. Understanding how people behave with money? That can take decades.

Here's what I noticed: more than 90% of working people don't have a practical financial blueprint. They chase shiny objects—cars, trips, gadgets—while ignoring the life-changing disciplines of saving, investing, and building assets.

If that sounds like you, don't panic. You're not broken. You're simply running a program that no longer serves you. And once the right motivation clicks, change is possible.

When Money Destroys

I've also witnessed the darker side of money:

- **Big spenders** with massive houses, luxury cars, and "everything" can go bankrupt spectacularly—not because they earned too little, but because they lost respect for money's purpose: security, freedom, and choice.
- **Greedy promoters** exaggerate returns, push schemes, and manipulate others' savings. They make money fast—but almost without exception, they pay a personal price later: broken marriages, health crises, ruined reputations.

It made me wonder: is there financial karma? Do those who put money above people eventually pay the price? From what I've seen—the answer leans yes.

The Limits of Financial Advice

Here's a hard truth: **your financial advisor will not make you rich.**

I know—I was one. Advisors play a crucial role: managing risk, keeping you legally compliant, and guiding investments under their license (superannuation, managed funds, approved equities).

What they **cannot** do is guide you toward real wealth: property, businesses, private equity, cryptocurrency, or unconventional assets. The system is designed for **safety, not wealth creation**.

To build serious wealth, you must:
- Educate yourself
- Think like an investor
- Take calculated risks

Stuart's Turning Point

One story illustrates this perfectly.

Stuart, a business broker, was on the verge of financial collapse. Deals weren't closing. Cash flow was drying up. He came to me expecting a financial strategy. Instead, I told him:

"Stuart, start giving money away. Buy something for someone who matters. Hand cash to someone in need. Give first."

He was stunned. "I'm broke. And you want me to give money away?"

"Yes," I said. "Because giving shifts your energy. It shows trust. And right now, you have little to lose."

Two days later, he gave a distressed woman six dollars. The next morning, two prospective clients he'd been chasing for months called back. Together, they committed over $60,000 in business.

Giving didn't cost Stuart—it **catalyzed growth**. From that day forward, his business, reputation, and confidence soared.

Lesson: Wealth isn't just numbers—it's mindset, respect, and energy.

The Wealth Paradox

Money amplifies who you are:
- Careless → accelerated downfall
- Greedy → exposed emptiness
- Respectful → opens doors

Wealth begins with mindset. Stuart's story proves that generosity, discipline, and focus are as important as strategy or capital.

Shifting From Employee to Investor

Most people think like employees: hours, paychecks, promotions. Wealthy people think like investors: assets, equity, leverage.
- Employee mindset: "Can I afford this car?"
- Investor mindset: "What asset can I acquire that will pay for this car?"

One mindset keeps you dependent. The other sets you free.

Mentors, Models, and Decisions

If advisors can't make you wealthy, who can?
- **Mentors:** people who've done it and know the real game
- **Models:** proven strategies to study and adapt
- **Decisions:** the daily choices you make, the risks you're willing to take

Wealth leaves clues. But only you can follow them.

Mindset Is Your First Asset

Your most valuable financial asset isn't money—it's your mindset.

- Spender blueprint → you'll spend everything you touch
- Investor blueprint → you'll multiply everything you touch

Some start with little and build empires; others inherit millions and lose it within a decade. Mindset determines outcomes long before the bank account does.

Chapter Summary — 5 Key Takeaways

1. **Money amplifies you.** Without a practical financial blueprint, sudden wealth disappears.
2. **Advisors manage; they don't multiply.** Their job is safety, not wealth creation.
3. **Real wealth requires risk.** Property, business, and innovation carry uncertainty—but also opportunity.
4. **Shift from employee to investor thinking.** Build assets that outlive your labor.
5. **Giving unlocks growth.** Generosity shifts energy, attracts opportunity, and rewires your relationship with money.

Chapter 9:
The Importance of Sales & Marketing

Decisions Determine Destiny

> *"Decisions determine destiny."*
>
> — Tony Robbins
>
> *"Profits are better than wages. Wages make you a living, profits make you a fortune."*
>
> — Jim Rohn

For years, I believed talent, hard work, and dedication alone would lead to success. I learned the uncomfortable truth: **talent without visibility is invisible.**

You can be brilliant at what you do, but if people don't understand your value—or worse, don't even know you exist—you'll struggle. Sales and marketing aren't side skills. They are the heartbeat of growth. Without them, even the best ideas die in silence.

The Pain of Confusion

Every day, talented professionals lose opportunities—not because they lack ability, but because their message is unclear:
- Marketing attracts attention—but not the right clients.
- Sales conversations linger—but don't close.
- Competitors with less skill win deals simply because they are clearer.

Confusion kills conversion. And confusion always costs more than clarity.

My Wake-Up Call

Early in my career, I thought talent alone would be rewarded. But the market doesn't reward the best-kept secret—it rewards the best-communicated value.

The moment I committed to mastering sales and marketing, everything changed. I stopped seeing sales as something I had to do and started seeing it as **something I got to do**. Selling became service. I wasn't convincing people; I was helping them make decisions that served their future.

That mental shift didn't just improve results—it multiplied them.

Gary's Breakthrough

Gary, a real estate agent, earned around $80,000 a year. Financial stress was crushing his marriage, and he was exhausted, stuck, and losing hope.

Through my workshop, he rethought his positioning. He realized his heritage gave him trust within a network of accountants. By clarifying his message and building referral partnerships, he transformed his business.

Within two years:

- Income skyrocketed to $650,000
- Marriage repaired
- Sense of possibility expanded

Gary didn't become more talented. He became more influential. That's the difference **sales and marketing make**.

Sales as Service

Sales isn't something you do to people—it's something you do **for** them.

When you adopt this mindset:
- Pressure disappears
- Objections become opportunities to listen and serve
- Selling becomes leadership: showing what's possible and giving courage to step into it

The Three Pillars of Influence

Influence drives results. Master it through three pillars:
1. **Clarity of Message** – Can you explain who you help, how, and the results in 30 seconds?
2. **Energy of Delivery** – Do you communicate with conviction, passion, and presence?
3. **Necessity of Action** – Do people walk away feeling working with you is essential, not optional?

When these pillars align, you stop chasing opportunities—they start seeking you.

The Funnel of Trust

A sales funnel is simply a **trust-building process**:
1. **Awareness** – People discover you
2. **Engagement** – They resonate with your story, values, or message
3. **Conversion** – They feel safe and ready to say yes

Skipping steps leads to desperate marketing and forced sales. Build trust step by step—clear message, genuine engagement, confident close—and growth becomes steady, scalable, and predictable.

Lessons From the Field

Biggest shifts in influence are simple:
1. **Simplify your message** – People can't buy what they don't understand
2. **Position yourself as the obvious choice** – Compete on authority, not price
3. **Follow up relentlessly** – Most sales happen after the fifth touchpoint
4. **Sell the transformation** – Don't sell services, sell the future outcome people crave

These small shifts create massive acceleration.

Turning Points in Sales

Breakthroughs in sales often begin with a decision:
- Stop avoiding sales
- See marketing as leadership
- Own your worth instead of apologizing

Each decision changes results instantly.

From Invisible to Irresistible

Master sales and marketing, and you move from invisible to irresistible.
- Stop being overlooked, start being sought
- Referrals multiply
- Income stabilizes and scales

Not because you became more talented, but because you became clearer, more confident, and intentional.

The world doesn't reward silence—it rewards clarity.

Growth With Integrity

Mastering influence doesn't mean being pushy or fake. It means **becoming more of who you already are**—clearer, bolder, and committed to serving others.

Do it with integrity:
1. Get clear on your message
2. Deliver it with energy
3. Show why action now matters
4. Lead with value first
5. Build trust at every step

Alignment drives results. When your message matches your mission, people feel it—and respond.

Chapter Summary — Top 5 Takeaways

1. Sales and marketing are the engine of growth. Without them, talent is invisible.
2. Clarity beats talent. If people don't understand your value, they can't buy from you.
3. Sales is service. Helping people decide confidently is leadership in action.
4. Influence has three pillars: clarity, energy, and necessity. Master them to attract clients.
5. Your next income level depends on one shift: stop avoiding sales, start embracing influence.

Final Word

Stop hiding behind your ability. Lead with clarity.

Sales and marketing are **not about pressure—they are about service, influence, and trust.** Master them, and you don't just increase income—you expand impact, create momentum, and unlock opportunities that were previously invisible.

The better you communicate your value, the faster the world responds.

Chapter 10:
Success Leaves Clues
—Here's How to Follow Them

Spend time around the top 1%—elite business leaders, championship athletes, or renowned creatives—and you'll notice something subtle but undeniable: **they operate by a different rhythm.**

It's not luck. It's not rare DNA. And it's not simply intelligence (though many are smart). The truth? They practice **behaviours so consistently that they become their identity.**

The good news: behaviours can be learned. When you model them, you get the same leverage they do.

After decades of coaching high performers, I've distilled what separates the elite from the average into **four behaviours**—simple habits almost no one applies consistently:

1. Decisive
2. Finishers
3. Goal-driven and reflective
4. Continuous learners

Let's break them down.

1. Decisive: Success Loves Speed

Most people live in the "waiting room" of life—waiting for certainty, money, time, or validation. The top 1% don't. They decide, move, and course-correct later.

Every breakthrough starts with a decision: leaving a job, pursuing a client, or investing in yourself. Without decisions, nothing changes.

Elon Musk is a prime example. He doesn't sit on ideas for years. He tests, builds, and refines—decisiveness keeps him ahead.

How to apply it:

- Set deadlines for decisions: 24 hours for small choices, 7 days for big ones.
- Ask: "What's the next step I can decide on today that creates momentum?"
- Shift your mindset: "What if it works?" instead of "What if it fails?"

Decisiveness isn't arrogance—it's **trust in yourself to move.**

2. Finish What You Start

Chronic starters never win. Half-written books, unfinished businesses, unkept gym routines—they drain mental energy and slow progress.

The top 1% finish. Big or small, they close the loop. Completion frees mental bandwidth, builds momentum, and reinforces trust in themselves.

I worked with a consultant brilliant at ideas but terrible at execution. Once he committed to finishing projects, client trust grew, revenue stabilized, and his confidence soared.

How to apply it:

- Create a "finish list" weekly—track completions, not just starts.
- Limit projects. Finish one before starting another.
- Celebrate completions to reinforce the habit.

Being a finisher isn't flashy—but it's **magnetic and trustworthy.**

3. Goals: Set, Track, Review

Most people set goals annually—and forget them by March. The 1% treat goal-setting like **oxygen**.

High performers:

- Write goals down
- Break them into milestones
- Review weekly
- Adjust with life changes

Goals are **compasses, not checklists.** Without them, you drift; with them, you direct.

A CEO client coasting in his business rebuilt his weekly routine around goal review. Within a year, revenue grew 38%—not magic, but consistent focus.

How to apply it:

- Write your top 3 goals on a card and carry it everywhere
- Weekly reflection: "What moved me closer this week?" "What will I do next week?"
- Share with a peer or mentor for accountability Goals aren't pressure—they're **focus**.

4. Continuous Learning: Stay Sharp, Stay Relevant

The world doesn't care what you knew last year—or five years ago. If you're not learning, you're falling behind.

The 1% **never stop learning**. Seminars, masterminds, books—they absorb knowledge intentionally, applying it to stay relevant and ahead.

Warren Buffett reads 5–6 hours daily. Bill Gates takes "think weeks." Different methods, same principle: learning = competitive advantage.

How to apply it:

- Read 30 minutes daily; even one book a month keeps you ahead
- Curate your inputs: growth over gossip
- Teach what you learn—sharing deepens mastery

Continuous learning keeps your **brain agile, perspective fresh, and opportunities expanding.**

The Feedback Loop of Mastery

These four behaviours compound:
- Decisiveness → more completions
- Completions → momentum and goal reinforcement
- Goal review → clarity on what to learn next
- Learning → sharper, faster decisions

It's a **self-reinforcing cycle** that pushes you upward. The 1% stay ahead—not because of talent, but because their behaviours compound.

Your Challenge: Audit Your 1% Behaviours

Score yourself 1–10 in each area:
- **Decisiveness:** Do I make clear, timely decisions or procrastinate?
- **Completion:** Do I finish what I start, big and small?
- **Goals:** Do I set, track, and review goals regularly?
- **Learning:** Am I consistently learning and applying new ideas?

Your lowest score is your leverage point. Start there, and the rest rises.

Chapter Summary — 5 Key Takeaways

1. The top 1% aren't magical—they're methodical.
2. Decisiveness creates momentum; waiting kills it.
3. Completion builds confidence and trust; finish everything you start.
4. Goals are compasses, not optional; set, review, and live by them.
5. Continuous learning keeps you sharp, relevant, and resilient.

Success leaves clues. Model these behaviours consistently, and you'll stop chasing success—and start **living it.**

Chapter 11:
How to Reclaim Your Energy in a Distracted World Drowning in Distraction

Most people don't fail because they lack talent. They fail because their energy is scattered across a thousand tiny interruptions. They don't collapse from exhaustion—they bleed out from distraction.

We live in the noisiest era of human history. The volume knob on life is stuck at maximum. The world constantly pings, buzzes, vibrates, and demands something from you. In this environment, clarity isn't optional—it's survival.

Top performers know this. They understand that without protected focus, **everything else suffers**: work, health, relationships, and happiness.

The paradox: it's not the big crises that derail us. It's the endless stream of tiny distractions that slowly drains our power.

The Five Horsemen of Distraction

Here are the top five distractions destroying your productivity—and your peace of mind:

1. **Loud Noise** – Traffic, construction, or a blaring TV hijacks attention. Noise drains cognitive energy; your brain can only process so much before fatigue sets in.
2. **Mobile Phones** – The biggest focus-killer of our time. Notifications, endless scrolling, and social media hits are designed to keep you hooked. The average person checks their phone **over 90 times a day**. That's not connection—it's addiction.
3. **Unexpected Interruptions** – One "Got a minute?" can derail your flow. It can take up to **23 minutes** to fully regain focus after an interruption. Ten such interruptions a day? Hours lost.

4. **Energy Drainers** – People who constantly complain, interrupt, or thrive on chaos steal more than your time—they drain your mental energy and leave residual clutter long after they're gone.
5. **Shortened Attention Spans** – Constant stimulation from TikTok, YouTube Shorts, or rapid-fire media weakens your mental muscle for sustained focus.

These aren't minor inconveniences—they're **silent killers of potential.**

The War Inside Your Mind

Distraction isn't just external—it's internal.

Your mind has two key functions:

- **Logical Mind** – Craves order, structure, and progress. Sets goals, makes lists, loves clarity.
- **Emotional Mind** – Reactive, impulsive, and mostly in charge. Reaches for the phone when bored, checks email mid-task, or "busies" itself to avoid discomfort.

Most believe they're logical creatures who occasionally get emotional. Reality: **we're emotional creatures who occasionally manage to be logical.**

Focus doesn't happen by default. It's engineered. You must **train your environment and habits** to protect your logical mind from hijacking by your emotional mind.

The Cost of Noise

Every distraction comes at a price—not just lost minutes, but lost momentum.

- How many brilliant ideas were cut off mid-thought by a buzzing phone?
- How many projects were delayed due to others' crises?
- How many workouts, conversations, or creative breakthroughs were sabotaged by noise?

The cost isn't just time—it's **wasted potential.**

How High Performers Protect Focus

Elite performers make distraction the exception, not the rule. Here's how:

1. **Silence the Environment** – Noise-cancelling headphones, closed doors, dedicated quiet spaces. They don't wait for peace—they **build it.**
2. **Dominate the Phone** – Notifications off. Do Not Disturb during deep work. Social media apps were removed from the home screen. The phone becomes a **tool, not a leash.**
3. **Block Interruptions** – Schedule "office hours." Signal deep work mode with visual cues (like a red wristband). Train teams and family to respect boundaries.
4. **Set Energy Boundaries** – Spend less time with complainers, more with encouragers. Who you spend time with either fuels your focus or fractures it.
5. **Train Attention Like a Muscle** – Read books instead of skimming articles. Write for 25 minutes without phone distractions. Meditate. Push your brain to sustain attention longer. Focus **grows stronger with use.**

The Freedom of Focus

Focus isn't restriction—it's freedom.

When you control your focus, you control your energy. Control your energy, and you control your life. You choose **what gets your attention**, set standards, and live deliberately instead of reactively.

This is why high performers accomplish in a year what others struggle with for a decade.

Your Action Plan to Kill the Noise

1. **Audit Your Distractions** – Write down your top three daily distractions. Awareness is the first step.
2. **Control the Phone** – Turn off non-essential notifications. Create a daily "phone-free zone" (e.g., first hour after waking, last hour before bed).
3. **Create Deep Work Rituals** – Block 90 minutes daily for focused work. No interruptions, no excuses.
4. **Guard Your Energy** – Minimise time with chronic distractors. Maximise time with those who elevate you.
5. **Train Your Focus Muscle** – Start small: 10 minutes of reading without checking your phone. Build gradually.

Chapter Summary — Top 5 Takeaways

1. Distraction is the silent killer of progress. It's not talent you lack—it's clarity.
2. Five major distractions: noise, phones, interruptions, energy drainers, and shortened attention spans.
3. Your logical mind craves order, but your emotional mind controls most reactions. Discipline protects clarity.
4. High performers don't hope for focus—they **engineer it** through systems, environment, and habits.
5. Focus isn't restriction—it's freedom. Reclaiming attention means reclaiming energy, time, and potential.

Final Word

The world isn't going to get quieter—but you can. Focus isn't about doing more—it's about deciding what matters and cutting everything else.

High performers rise above the noise not because they're smarter or luckier—they're ruthless about protecting their focus. You can be too.

Clarity isn't just power—it's your ultimate advantage.

Chapter 12:
A Simple Daily Reset for Confidence, Clarity, and Calm Before the World Gets to You, Get to Yourself

Most people don't lose their day because they lack ambition. They lose it in the **first ten minutes after waking**.

They reach for their phones, scroll through emails, and let notifications dictate their priorities. Suddenly, their mind is **running on someone else's agenda** before they've even taken a breath.

High performers do the opposite. They start their mornings **with intention**, grounding themselves, clarifying focus, and priming energy before the world rushes in. That's why a consistent morning ritual is one of the **most powerful tools for momentum**.

And here's the secret: it doesn't have to take an hour of yoga, green juice, and journaling. You can **reset your state of mind in just seven minutes** if done deliberately.

The Purpose of a Morning Ritual

The morning ritual isn't another item on your to-do list. It's **space before the noise**, a daily reboot. It's your chance to **claim ownership of your mind** before others hijack it.

The 7-Minute Framework

Seven minutes, five deliberate practices, each designed to **sharpen clarity, calm emotions, and set direction**:

1. **One Minute of Breathing and Stillness:** Sit or stand with eyes closed. Inhale deeply through your nose, hold for a few seconds, then exhale slowly. Repeat for a full minute. This isn't about

clearing thoughts—it's about **allowing mental noise to settle**, pressing the reset button on your nervous system.

2. **Two Minutes of Gratitude and Reflection**: Name three specific things you're grateful for: a person, a recent win, even the simple fact that you're alive. Gratitude **interrupts negativity bias** and primes your mind to see possibilities instead of problems.
3. **Two Minutes of Visualisation and Goal Review**: Picture moving through your day with confidence and focus. Visualise completing your most important task. Review your top 2–3 goals—not a giant to-do list, but the outcomes that matter most. This **aligns your actions with your vision**.
4. **One Minute of Affirmations**: Speak or silently repeat identity-based statements that reinforce who you want to become. Affirmations anchor your subconscious to the standards you aim to live by. Examples include:
    o "I choose clarity over chaos."
    o "I focus on the most profitable actions first."
    o "Each day I am stronger, wiser, and more confident."
5. **One Minute of Movement**: Stretch, do push-ups, or simply roll your shoulders back and stand tall. **Energy in the body creates energy in the mind.**

Seven minutes. No apps. No equipment. Just **you, your breath, and focus**.

The Death of the To-Do List

Most productivity advice glorifies to-do lists—but they're a trap.

To-do lists look productive but are rarely effective. They're endless, overwhelming, and filled with low-value tasks that **keep you busy but not impactful**.

High performers don't ask, "What's on my list today?" They ask,

"What matters most? What's most profitable?"

Shift to a **priority schedule**:
- A to-do list = a random collection of tasks.
- A priority schedule = ranked top 3 outcomes for the day, with dedicated time to complete them.

Example: If sales drive your business, **client calls come first**, not tweaking a website. If health matters, **exercise and meal prep take priority**.

Rule: **Do the most profitable or meaningful thing first.** Profit can be financial, relational, or personal—it must **compound in value.**

Mindfulness: Rest and Refresh Your Mind

Performance isn't just about doing—it's also about **mental recovery**.

Without mindfulness, your brain never truly rests. Emails, decisions, conversations, and media inputs accumulate. By the evening, you feel drained but unproductive.

Mindfulness isn't mystical. It's **a tool for cognitive clarity**. Just one to five minutes of daily breathing **lowers stress hormones, sharpens focus, and strengthens intentional responses**.

Mindfulness builds space between stimulus and response. Instead of being reactive, your **logical mind takes the driver's seat**.

The Two Minds at War

You live with two minds:
1. **Logical Mind** – Plans, organises, and thrives on clarity.
2. **Emotional Mind** – Reactive, seeks comfort, and often drives behaviour without permission.

Most assume they're logical, but reality: **emotions often run the show**.

The morning ritual **flips the switch**. Logic leads; emotion follows. Breathing, gratitude, visualisation, and affirmations **prime your mind to lead with reason, not reaction.**

Why Small Wins Matter

Seven minutes might seem trivial—but **small wins compound**.

Starting the day with control, clarity, and energy sets the tone for everything else. Over time, consistency separates the overwhelmed from the unstoppable.

Your Action Plan

1. **Commit to 7 Minutes Daily** – Before checking your phone.
2. **Replace To-Do Lists with Priority Schedules** – Focus on your three most profitable actions and block time for them.
3. **Practice Mindfulness** – One to five minutes of deliberate breathing.
4. **Use Affirmations** – Anchor your subconscious with identity-based truths.
5. **Finish What You Start** – Avoid incomplete tasks bleeding your energy.

Chapter Summary — Top 5 Takeaways

1. Morning rituals build momentum. Seven minutes can **change your day's trajectory**.
2. To-do lists are traps. Replace them with **priority schedules** focused on profit and purpose.
3. Your mind has two functions. Without mindfulness, the emotional mind hijacks your day.
4. Affirmations align identity. Use them to **reprogram beliefs and anchor confidence**.
5. Small daily wins lead to long-term mastery. Rituals aren't about perfection—they're about **momentum.**

Final Word

You don't need a two-hour routine or complicated productivity hacks. You need **seven intentional minutes** to claim your mind before the world does.

Kill the noise. Focus on what matters. Success is rarely about doing more—it's about **doing the right things first, with clarity and consistency**.

Your morning sets the foundation of your life. Protect it, and everything else will rise.

CHAPTER 13:
The Quiet Truth About High Achievers

The people who rise to the top in business, sports, and life aren't smarter, luckier, or immune to failure.

What sets the 1% apart from the 99% is a handful of **character traits**—traits I call the **Relentless Code**.

They're deceptively simple: **desire, faith, inspired action, and persistence.** When practiced daily, they can bend the trajectory of your life.

Napoleon Hill called these traits "indispensable" in *Think and Grow Rich*. Jim Rohn reminded us, *"To have more or do more, you first have to BECOME more."*

Every person I've coached who has made a significant leap in wealth, influence, or personal growth has embodied this code in some form.

Desire: The Spark That Lights Everything

Nothing begins without **desire**.

Desire is not a vague wish. It's not *"I'd like more money"* or *"I'd like to be healthier."* True desire is **specific, measurable, and burning enough to withstand setbacks**.

Hill wrote, *"Every fortune begins with a burning desire for definite riches."* That burning desire:

- Pushes you out of bed early
- Keeps you in the game when others quit
- Makes sacrifices feel natural, because nothing else compares to the outcome

Most people let life dull their desire. They confuse comfort with success and settle for "good enough." Desire requires courage—it asks you to admit, *"I want more."*

Want more money. Want more health. Want more fulfilling relationships.

Desire isn't greed—it's growth.

Faith: The Invisible Fuel

Desire without **faith** is just daydreaming.

Faith is **belief in advance of evidence**. It keeps you moving when there's no visible proof that your actions will work.

Faith is not blind optimism. It's a **decision to bet on yourself**, trusting that persistence and integrity will eventually be rewarded.

Every breakthrough in my career started with faith. I had no guarantees:

- That a breakfast meeting would lead to deals
- That a seminar would catapult my income
- That investing in my education would pay off

Faith says: *"Even if I can't see the path clearly, every step forward matters."*

Inspired Action: Moving Beyond "Busy"

Most people mistake motion for progress.

They fill calendars, tick boxes, and look busy—but **busyness is not productivity**.

Inspired action is different. It is:

- Aligned
- Purposeful
- Bold (often uncomfortable)

It's the call you make to a client you've been avoiding. It's hiring help to free yourself from low-value tasks. It's investing in a mentor who will push you further.

Each act of inspired action **shifts your identity**: *"This is who I am now. This is the standard I live by."*

Persistence: The Quiet Superpower

Desire starts the journey. Faith fuels it. Inspired action moves you.

Persistence gets you there.

Success often takes longer than expected. Setbacks happen: deals fall through, clients leave, markets shift.

The winners aren't those who never fail—they're those who **never stop**.

Persistence is a daily choice:
- Recommit even when yesterday didn't deliver
- Treat rejection as feedback, not finality
- Recognize that every "no" brings you closer to the transformative "yes"

The Big Secret of High Achievers

Top performers—CEOs, elite athletes, authors, entrepreneurs—**all have mentors and coaches**.
- Athletes have coaches for mindset, strategy, and strength.
- CEOs rely on boards of advisors and peer groups.
- Top authors and speakers surround themselves with guides who challenge and refine them.

Even the most driven people have **blind spots**. They can't always see their own excuses or patterns. Coaches and mentors provide:

- Perspective
- Accountability
- Tough truths you might avoid

Think of persistence as the engine—coaches are the mechanics keeping it tuned for the long haul.

The Two Types of Pain

Gary Ryan Blair says: *"Everything you want in life comes with a price tag. That price is suffering."*

You get to choose your pain:

1. **The pain of discipline:** showing up early, having the tough conversation, sacrificing comfort
2. **The pain of regret:** looking back on years lost because you didn't act boldly

Mentors tilt you toward **discipline** and away from **regret**. **Real-World Shifts**

These principles transform lives:

- **The Overworked Consultant:** Doubled her rates, redefined her identity as a premium advisor
- **The Struggling Entrepreneur:** Hired a mentor, implemented a new sales system, landed three high-ticket clients in 30 days
- **The Plateaued CEO:** Sought a new peer group, redefined standards, and broke through stagnation

Pattern: Those who embody the Relentless Code and surround themselves with mentors **outpace those who go it alone.**

Your Turn: Living the Relentless Code

Start today:
1. **Clarify Desire:** Write exactly what you want in the next 12 months. Be specific.
2. **Strengthen Faith:** Create a daily affirmation reinforcing belief in your outcome.
3. **Take Inspired Action:** Identify the bold move you've been avoiding—complete it within 48 hours.
4. **Commit to Persistence:** Pick one habit to repeat daily for the next 90 days, no matter what.
5. **Find a Mentor:** Stop going it alone. Hire a coach, join a mastermind, or surround yourself with challengers.

Chapter Summary: 5 Key Takeaways

1. Desire is the starting line—without it, nothing happens.
2. Faith keeps you steady when results aren't yet visible.
3. Inspired action is the antidote to busyness—do what matters most.
4. Persistence is a superpower—winners keep going when others quit.
5. Every high achiever has mentors and coaches. Success is **never a solo sport.**

Final Word

The Relentless Code isn't glamorous—but it works.
- **Desire** lights the fire
- **Faith** keeps it burning
- **Action** fans the flames
- **Persistence** carries you through storms
- **Mentors** make sure you don't burn out or lose your way

When practiced consistently, the Relentless Code **reshapes your life, your habits, and your results.**

Chapter 14:
Your Defining Moment

Your Story Doesn't End Here

Every book ends. But your story doesn't.

The words you've read across these chapters will fade unless you do something about them—**today, not "someday."**

Here's the truth no one likes to hear: transformation isn't about how much you know. It's about **what you do with what you know**. And if you've come this far, you already know enough to change everything.

What separates the 1% from the 99% isn't knowledge, luck, or talent. It's **a decision**—a final, non-negotiable decision to live differently, think differently, and act differently.

This is no longer just a book you read. It's your line in the sand.

The Myth of More Time

Too many people treat personal growth like a spectator sport.

- They buy courses.
- They fill notebooks.
- They highlight paragraphs.

And then quietly drift back to old patterns, waiting for Monday, January 1st, the kids to grow up, or the economy to turn.

Decades of working with CEOs, advisors, and professionals have taught me one truth: **waiting is the slowest form of suicide.**

The longer you wait, the heavier the boulder grows. The braver choice is to **act now**, before comfort whispers you back into mediocrity.

The Lesson of Serendipity

Looking back, the turning points of my life never came with fanfare or neon signs. They looked like coincidences:

- A chance meeting at a party opened a career door.
- A seminar I almost skipped rewired my thinking.
- A casual five-minute conversation with a mentor shifted my trajectory.

At first glance, these moments seemed random. But they weren't. They were proof of a bigger principle: **when you raise your standards and decide to grow, opportunities appear, and the right people come into your life.**

And it's not just business. Serendipity brings vibrancy back into life. It introduces new people, perspectives, and possibilities that feel alive, expansive, even spectacular.

The only condition? You must **be open to them.** You can't script them. You can't predict them. But you can **recognize, embrace, and act** when they appear.

The Final Secret of Success

Here's something high achievers rarely announce: **they all have mentors and coaches.**

- Every elite athlete.
- Every top executive.
- Every serious wealth creator.

They stack their environment with people who pull them forward, challenge blind spots, and hold them accountable.

You can't see your own programming clearly enough to rewrite it alone. You need an outside perspective—a mirror, a guide, a challenger.

A Real-World Example: Chris

Chris started as a humble accountant in Melbourne, comfortable in a steady career. But he knew staying comfortable wouldn't unleash his potential.

We worked together from day one: mindset, confidence, and leadership in a high-stakes environment. He didn't just want a job— he wanted to contribute at the highest level.

Chris listened, absorbed, and applied. He carried himself with integrity and relentless dedication. Within three years, he was offered **equity partnership** in one of Melbourne's most prestigious property development companies. Today, he's a **$100 million entrepreneur with over $1 million monthly income.**

The secret? He raised his standards, leaned into mentorship, and delivered with excellence.

High achievers aren't walking alone—they're plugged into mentors, peers, and guides who constantly expand what's possible.

Your Call to Action

Here's my challenge to you:
1. **Choose ONE thing** from this book that resonated with you most.
2. Decide to apply it within 24 hours.
3. **Tell someone**—a colleague, spouse, or mentor—what you're committing to.

Not five things. Not ten. Just one. Momentum comes from doing **something that matters** and letting that energy compound.

Chapter Summary — 5 Key Takeaways

1. Knowledge without action is dead weight. Your power lies in execution.
2. Waiting for the "right time" is the enemy. **The right time is now.**
3. Serendipity is real—life-changing opportunities appear when you're **open and alert**.
4. Every elite performer has mentors. **Find yours** to accelerate results.
5. The decision you make today can become the **turning point of your life**.

Final Word

This book isn't the end. It's your beginning.

Somewhere out there is the conversation that will change your trajectory, the opportunity that will shift your future, the person who will raise your standards. But you don't stumble into them by staying the same.

Raise your standards. Make your decision. Step into the arena.

Your transformation begins the moment you say:

"Enough. I choose more."

The Life Success Accelerator

Are you ready to **live the life you deserve**?

Did this book spark something in you—an idea, a feeling, a realization that you're ready for more?

If so, I'd like to personally invite you to take the next step with me.

The Life Success Accelerator is your chance to go beyond reading and actually **live these principles**. This powerful coaching experience will help you:

- Gain **clarity and momentum** in your personal and professional life.
- Connect with **like-minded individuals** who, just like you, want to grow, succeed, and live with purpose.
- Focus on the areas that matter most:
    - **Income & Career** – unlocking new levels of opportunity and growth.
    - **Business & Wealth** – creating stability and momentum.
    - **Relationships** – building deeper connections and trust.
    - **Mindset & Mental Clarity** – reclaiming energy and focus.

You don't have to do this alone. True breakthroughs happen when you **surround yourself with the right guidance and the right people.**

My Gift to You

To help you get started, I'm offering a **complimentary strategy call (valued at $497)**. In this call, you'll gain clarity, direction, and **specific steps you can implement immediately** to start transforming your life.

You have nothing to lose—and a life of possibility to gain.

Let's Begin

If you're ready to stop waiting and start living the life you know you're capable of, I'd love to connect with you personally:

Email: businessprofitgrowth@gmail.com

Phone: +61 0421 781 242

LinkedIn: DM me directly

The journey starts with **one decision**. Say yes to yourself, and let's make this the turning point you'll look back on for years to come.

It's time to rise. It's time to accelerate.

Recommended Resources

These are the authors, mentors, and works that shaped my thinking and refined the principles inside *The Secrets to Instant Change*. Each one is a **powerful tool for growth**.

Foundational Thinkers & Mentors

- **Bob Proctor** — *You Were Born Rich*: Bob taught me that success comes from environment and standards, not innate ability. His lessons on self-image remain timeless.
- **Tony Robbins** — *Awaken the Giant Within*, *Unlimited Power*: Tony showed me that raising your standards is the single most important decision you'll ever make. His strategies for energy, mindset, and leadership are essential.
- **Dr. Robert Anthony** — *Beyond Positive Thinking*: Anthony exposed the limits of "positive thinking," teaching me that clarity, identity, and self-image are far more powerful than affirmations alone.
- **Eric Butterworth** — *Spiritual Economics*: A profound resource linking spiritual principles with prosperity. His perspective on abundance transformed how I give, receive, and live with purpose.

- **Jim Rohn** — *The Treasury of Quotes*, *The Art of Exceptional Living*: Jim's philosophy of daily discipline and personal responsibility is simple but profound.
- **W. Clement Stone** — *Success Through a Positive Mental Attitude*: Stone bridges mindset and measurable results, showing that optimism is a practical strategy, not just an attitude.

Modern Voices on Wealth & Growth

- **Morgan Housel** — *The Psychology of Money*: Housel distills finance to human behavior, showing why intelligence without emotional control fails.
- **T. Harv Eker** — *Secrets of the Millionaire Mind*: Eker reveals the subconscious "money blueprint" we inherit and how to rewire it for financial success.
- **Daniel Priestley** — *Key Person of Influence*, *Oversubscribed*: Priestley teaches how to stand out and scale by becoming the go-to person in your field.
- **Gary Ryan Blair** — *Everything Counts!*: Blair's frameworks show the compounding power of small disciplines for execution at the highest level.

Leadership & Business

- **Bob Iger** — *The Ride of a Lifetime*: A masterclass in leadership, decision-making, and resilience from the former Disney CEO.
- **Brendon Burchard** — *High Performance Habits*: Burchard shows how to systematize clarity, energy, and productivity.
- **Dan Kennedy** — *No B.S. Series*: A no-nonsense approach to marketing, wealth-building, and communicating value.
- **Eugene Schwartz** — *Breakthrough Advertising*: One of the greatest copywriters ever; teaches psychology, persuasion, and meeting audiences where they are.

Biographies & Personal Journeys

- **Andre Agassi — *Open: An Autobiography***: A brutally honest look at the life of a champion, identity struggles, and reinvention.
- **Dale Carnegie — *How to Win Friends and Influence People***: The classic on human connection, influence, and trust-building.

Podcasts & Interviews

- **Lewis Howes — *The School of Greatness***: Interviews with top performers across industries; a treasure trove of mindset, habits, and strategies.

www.ingramcontent.com/pod-product-compliance
Lightning Source LLC
Chambersburg PA
CBHW072203160426
43197CB00012B/2500